PAUL NEWMAN

A Life in Pictures Edited by Yann-Brice Dherbier & Pierre-Henri Verlhac

Rolex is gratefully acknowledged for its support of this project

CHRONICLE BOOKS

SAN FRANCISCO

Paul Newman

PAUL NEWMAN

A biography by Laurence Aiach

Paul Newman's long, storied life is a tale of hard work, determination, and integrity—along with good measure of plain old luck. Determined to take charge of his own life from an early age, Newman is a man who has never let anyone tell him what road to follow.

On January 26, 1925, as bitter winds howled off Lake Erie and thick snow blanketed the city of Cleveland, Theresa Newman gave birth to her second son, Paul Leonard. A handsome eight-pound baby, he dazzled everyone with his piercing blue eyes.

Paul grew up in a warm and loving atmosphere in his family's comfortable eleven-room home in Shaker Heights, a suburb of Cleveland. His father, Arthur, a popular, highly respected owner of a sporting goods store, was Jewish and of Hungarian-Polish origin. His mother, Theresa, came from an upper-class Roman Catholic family of Hungarian origin. The Newmans worked hard to instill the value of hard work, dignity, respect, and family loyalty in their two sons. Money, although it wasn't scarce, wasn't handed out but earned. Arthur and Theresa raised their children to become respectable members of society, with high moral standards. Paul's road was laid out before him: marry a girl from a good family, take over the family business, and assume his place as a pillar of the community.

It was Paul's uncle Joe who introduced him to a world beyond the confines of Shaker Heights. A journalist, lyricist, and poet, Joe introduced Paul to literature and a more unconventional lifestyle. Likewise, Paul's mother also unwittingly opened the door to acting. An impassioned theatergoer, Theresa regularly made trips into the city to attend plays, always giving Paul a detailed account of what she had seen. Encouraged by his mother, Paul took part in many school plays and joined a children's theater, The Curtain Raises. At seven, he played a court jester in *Robin Hood,* and delighted the audience with one of his Uncle Joe's songs. At ten, he played Saint George; the dragon was played by a ferocious bulldog. At ease on stage and not intimidated by an audience, Paul made his parents very proud.

Despite his ease in performing, Paul showed no particular vocation for acting as a child. No one, including himself, took his acting abilities seriously. Seen as a "promising student," he sailed through school and attracted the envy of his peers. Former classmates remember him as a charming youngster with a restrained intensity. Under a veneer of social grace, there were, perhaps, the first intimations of rebellion. Paul knew just how far he could go and where to draw the line.

Even as a child, Paul displayed uncommon intellectual gifts. There was nothing timid about him, and he understood how to hold public attention. He quickly became aware of the admiration his good looks inspired in those around him. In adolescence, while he was aware of the social advantages he held, he constantly guarded himself against vanity. He joined the debate team and emceed high school events, but his real love was sports—football, baseball, and basketball. He delivered his most spectacular battles on the playing field and dreamed of becoming a professional football player.

During summer vacations, Paul had a series of jobs, including selling encyclopedias door to door. He was acting already—charming clients and making record-breaking sales for a beginner. After graduating high school in 1943, he enlisted in the Navy. While waiting to be called up, he enrolled at Ohio University in Athens, Ohio, where he majored, he says, in "beer drinking."

In the Navy, Paul volunteered for pilot training and was selected for special training. He passed test after test, but his dream of becoming a pilot crumbled after it was discovered that he was color-blind. He was assigned instead to be a radio operator for the Pacific torpedo fleet.

During his Navy years, Paul had only one goal: to return to college. He absorbed everything that passed through his hands, reading between ten and fifteen books a week. In April 1946, he was finally released from the military and returned to his studies at Kenyon College in Ohio. But after his time in the Navy, Paul realized that studying bored him. Finding himself free of family and social conventions, he began to relax and enjoy himself—perhaps a little too much. He became a football hero, with an entourage of female fans.

In 1948, some members of the Kenyon football team got into a bar brawl with several local high-school students. The ensuing punishment resulted in Paul being kicked off the football team. In the absence of football, Paul turned his attention to the theater. He auditioned for *The Front Page* and won the lead role. For the first time, he found genuine pleasure in acting.

On graduation, Paul left to join a theater company in Williams Bay, Wisconsin. He began the season without intending to pursue a career in acting, but he soon found himself more and more interested in the process of staging and producing a play. In the autumn, Paul joined the Woodstock Players in Illinois, where he fell in love for the first time.

JACKIE WITTE

Her name was Jackie Witte. Playing alongside Paul in *John and Mary,* she dazzled him with her energetic personality, independence, sensitivity, and positive outlook. They were married in December 1949. By now, Paul, who was twenty-five years old, had performed in sixteen plays.

In 1950, Paul's father became gravely ill. Paul felt that duty obliged him to leave Woodstock and rejoin his parents, so he and Jackie moved to Shaker Heights. Paul took up the family business, becoming the businessman that he had never wanted to be. He was good at it, and business thrived, but as he describes it, "I was very successful at being something I was not. And that's the worst thing that can happen to a person."

Later that year, two events pushed Paul to let himself lead his life as he wished, rather than the life that was expected of him: the birth of his first son, Scott, and the death of his father. He sold the family business, left Shaker Heights, and moved Jackie and Scott to New Haven, Connecticut, where he enrolled in Yale University Drama School in the fall of 1951.

Paul studied directing and stage production with the goal of becoming an acting teacher. His talent and charm were clear to everyone who encountered him. His wife, Jackie, ever supportive, was certain that a great destiny awaited him. It was at Yale that talent scouts William Liebling and Audrey Wood spotted him, suggesting he contact them should he ever come to New York. He hesitated: he had not imagined becoming a full-time actor or his family living such a Bohemian lifestyle. Abandoning his studies to go to New York frightened him, but Jackie encouraged him to accept. He did, on one condition: if he had not succeeded at the end of one year, he would return to Yale.

NEW YORK

In the summer of 1952, the family moved to a small apartment on Long Island and awaited the birth of their second child. Each morning, Paul took the ferry to Manhattan in his only suit in search of acting roles. Jackie had given up her career to be a full-time mother, and money was tight.

It wasn't long before Paul made his first appearance on television as an old man in *The March of Time.* Soon thereafter, more parts came his way, and he snagged a regular role on *The Aldrich Family.*

Paul met up again with Liebling and Wood, who arranged a meeting with playwright William Inge. Paul auditioned and was assigned the lead role in Inge's play *Picnic.* The Pulitzer Prize–winning play was an enormous success on Broadway: the playbill was posted for fourteen months, and Paul was nominated by *Theatre World* as one of the most "Promising Personalities" of 1953. Acclaimed by the critics, Paul, at twenty-eight, finally realized that acting was his life.

It was in *Picnic* that he met another young actress, hired as an understudy—Joanne Woodward. As she would later recount, she hated him at first sight. In return, Paul perceived Joanne as just another actress in New York. Despite this disastrous mutual first impression, little by little, they became close friends.

But Paul had not yet achieved all that he wanted. Among his motivations for coming to New York was Lee Strasberg's prestigious acting school, the Actors Studio. By chance, he agreed to help an acquaintance by playing opposite her in her own audition, a scene from Tennessee Williams' *Battle of Angels.* While normally two juried auditions were required for admission, Paul was offered admission to the Actors Studio based on that performance alone.

At thirty, Paul Newman had achieved a life of financial and social ease, he had a happy family life, and he'd had success on Broadway and gained admission to the Actors Studio. He had

become a familiar face in East Coast theater circles, and while most actors now worked in films, Paul resisted the siren song of Hollywood. Convinced that he was not among the best actors of his generation, he was sure that any Hollywood career would not be long-lasting. Also, the idea of being "bought" by the Hollywood "dream machine" was not appealing to him. But when Warner Bros. offered Newman a seven-year contract, he found he couldn't refuse. He packed his bags, left Jackie and the children in New York, and set off to conquer Hollywood.

HOLLYWOOD

Living out of a motel near the Warner Bros. studios, Paul endured some of the most difficult trials of his life. The businessmen who auditioned him found him to be "transparent and non-existent in front of the camera." He surmised that the only things that counted in the movie business were a good physique and a photogenic face—talent didn't seem to matter much at all. Hollywood was an entertainment industry in which loyalty was rare; the press pounced on every rumor and could destroy talent as easily as it had been discovered. Newman found all the glamour, glitzy evening galas, and opulent houses superficial.

A few diehards had managed to resist the "dark side" of Hollywood, among them Humphrey Bogart and Kirk Douglas, who became a close friend of Paul's. Douglas gave Newman some sensible advice: "To survive, you have to develop a sort of awareness of everything you see and experience. You also have to be compassionate. This will happen when you understand that no one here is a genius. There are just talented people, some more talented than others, working for a medium in which, occasionally, everything flows in the same direction. The rest is luck. It's only luck that will get you going . . ." Newman also befriended another up-and-coming young actor, James Dean, who had the same clear-eyed view of Hollywood. Already the winds of revolution were blowing across the studios' lots. The "dream machine" was at the beginning of a new era, it just didn't know it yet. Among the other rebels were Montgomery Clift and Marlon Brando.

In 1954, Newman made his first film, *The Silver Chalice.* Though he had screen-tested for the part of Cal Trask in *East of Eden,* that part went to James Dean, launching the two young actors on very different paths. Chosen on the basis of his good looks, blue eyes, and resemblance to Marlon Brando, he played a Greek slave. It was a disastrous and humiliating experience, and Newman became more determined than ever to return to Broadway, where he had met with public and critical acclaim.

He was reunited with his family once more, and Paul and Jackie's third child, Stephanie, was born in 1955. Back on Broadway, Newman played Glenn Griffin in *The Desperate Hours,* which Humphrey Bogart had played in the movie version. The play ran for eight months. At thirty, Newman was now considered a heartthrob on Broadway. Dozens of women awaited him every night at the stage door. Yet his cinematic endeavor was less successful—when *The Silver Chalice* was finally released, it was a decided flop. Newman refused to see the final cut. He finally saw the film a few months later when *The Desperate Hours* was playing in Philadelphia, and he was taken to the cinema against his will by some friends. His contract with Warner Bros. obliged him to act in two or three films a year, and they now loaned him out to Metro-Goldwyn-Mayer.

In September 1955, just weeks before Paul Newman and James Dean were to begin shooting a television adaptation of Ernest Hemingway's *The Battler,* Dean was killed in a car accident. Newman wanted to cancel, but the producers begged him to take the lead role, which had been Dean's. He finally yielded to their pressure.

Following his performance in *The Battler,* producers approached Newman to play boxer Rocky Graziano in *Somebody Up There Likes Me,* another role initially offered to James Dean. It was the role he had been waiting for. He prepared for it with the discipline of an Olympic athlete. Graziano himself guided Newman through the process, and he spent day after day training, soaking up his character. When the film came out in 1956, he was compared to Marlon Brando once again, but Newman still refused to accept the association.

With the release of *Somebody Up There Likes Me,* Paul Newman's popularity soared. Adored by the public and flattered by critics, he rarely saw his family, who had remained on Long Island. It was as if there were two Pauls, though he resisted both: He didn't want to become a Hollywood legend, but he also felt he couldn't be the head of his family. Everything was moving too fast. Success, pressure from the studios, estrangement from his family, and his practically nonexistent private life fueled his dislike of Hollywood. He and Jackie had become strangers to one another. They no longer belonged to the same world—while Paul's sphere had expanded, Jackie's had contracted to her family. Their lives seemed to have taken entirely separate paths.

In Los Angeles, Newman caught up again with the young actress he had met a few years before in New York, Joanne Woodward. She too had come west to make movies, and was under contract to Twentieth Century Fox. The two old friends saw a lot of each other. Their vision of the world, their approach to their profession, their views of life were all so close that they scarcely dared to admit what they already knew—that they were in love.

DILEMMA

Born into a middle-class family in Thomasville, Georgia, on February 27, 1930, Joanne Woodward was the child of divorced parents. Unlike Paul, Joanne always knew that she wanted to act. After studying at Louisiana State University, she enrolled in the Actors Studio. She landed several television roles before feeling the pull of Hollywood. But unlike so many young actresses, she refused to become a pin-up girl or starlet.

Although their feelings for each other deepened, words such as infidelity, cheating, adultery, and divorce were not part of Paul's vocabulary. He was faced with the greatest dilemma of his life. Guided by his principles and his upbringing, he decided to stop seeing Joanne, and she, who did not want to be seen as a home-wrecker, agreed.

Paul returned to his family to help raise his children, but his heart wasn't in it. He played again on Broadway (in *The Desperate Hours*), but his profession no longer interested him. He was still under contract and had to play roles in whatever films his studio offered. Traveling between New York and Los Angeles, he became irritable and emotionally unsteady. His reputation as a reticent and difficult actor increased, reinforcing earlier comparisons with Brando. He began to take comfort in alcohol, and in July 1956, he was arrested for drunk driving and spent a night in jail.

Aware that his emotions were weighing him down, Newman consulted a psychiatrist and found analysis an eye-opening experience. He invested himself in therapy, determined to find equilibrium. Paul "the Battler" (for his 1955 role) regained his footing little by little, partly through the profession of acting itself. Lee Strasberg helped him look inward, and as he explored the roles he had played, he found himself. To his surprise, he realized that he was not a saint, a revelation that would have larger consequences than he ever could have imagined. He began to release himself from the yoke of his upbringing and to acknowledge his imperfections.

In *The Helen Morgan Story* (1957), he played the kind of role that he really enjoyed: a gangster born on the wrong side of the tracks who persists in trying to do good. And then he was then cast in another film: *The Long, Hot Summer.* It costarred the woman who made his heart beat faster: Joanne.

JOANNE WOODWARD

The Long, Hot Summer was the first time Joanne and Paul were partners on a film. As usual, Paul arrived on scene well in advance of the rest of the crew and profited from his relative anonymity in small-town Mississippi to soak up the accent, manners, and conversations of the locals. When the film crew arrived, his cover was blown. Paparazzi tried to photograph Paul and Joanne, now lovers, but the townspeople took it upon themselves to show the photographers the road out of town. After that, Paul and Joanne no longer tried to hide. They were in love, and discovering the happiness of working together.

It was Jackie who initiated a divorce, granted in Mexico in 1957. On January 29, 1958, Joanne and Paul were married in an intimate ceremony in Las Vegas. After honeymooning in England, they settled into a home on the Upper East Side of Manhattan. At last, Paul had regained peace. He had married the love of his life, declaring, "Without her, I would be nowhere, I would be nothing."

Crowned with success and popularity, Paul and Joanne became one of the most glamorous couples in film. Joanne had just won the Oscar for Best Actress for her role in *The Three Faces of Eve* (1957), and not long after Paul became the first American to win the performance prize at the Cannes Film Festival for *The Long, Hot Summer* (1958). Soon, Joanne was expecting their first child: Daughter Elinor (Nell Potts) was born in 1959.

In 1958, Newman agreed to play Billy the Kid in *The Left Handed Gun*. Written by his friend Gore Vidal, the film cast the actor in the role of a nervous, psychotic character. Although the film was poorly received, the experience confirmed Newman's choice to continue playing antiheroes—misunderstood rebel characters were made for him.

Then, Newman was offered the role that would install him in the pantheon of Hollywood stars: *Cat on a Hot Tin Roof* (1958), co-starring Elizabeth Taylor. At the time this combative, emotionally wringing Tennessee Williams' drama was considered a shocking project—and that was all it took to get him to agree.

The shooting took place in Mississippi. Everyone held their breath—any rumor of amorous relations between the lead couple would have been a fabulous story. Unfortunately for the tabloids, Elizabeth was married to Mike Todd, whom she loved passionately, and Paul was married to his soul mate.

Halfway through the shooting, drama struck: Mike Todd was killed in an airplane crash over New Mexico. Elizabeth Taylor was devastated. From that point forward, Newman and Taylor poured themselves into their roles body and soul. When the shooting was over, they knew the film would be a success. And it was: *Cat on a Hot Tin Roof* won six Oscar nominations. Paul Newman had become cinematic gold.

PAUL NEWMAN, ICON

A Western, a comedy, a drama, a thriller, or a historic epic— Newman could play anything from a cop to a thug, a lover, an alcoholic, a cowboy, a rebel, or a troubled soul. His sculpted features, blue eyes, and charisma had turned him into an icon and a sex symbol.

Paul Newman's roles continued to confirm his talent and increase his popularity. In 1960, in the role of Ari Ben Canaan, he seemed to burst out of *Exodus*. A year later, he played tired hero and billiards legend "Fast" Eddie Felson in *The Hustler*. In 1963, he portrayed the kind of character he loved so much: a notorious alcoholic and debauched brawler in *Hud*. In *Hombre* he played another emblematic and nonconforming character, half Apache, half white. "Hombre means MAN . . . Paul is HOMBRE!" the trailer proclaimed. He appeared again in 1967 in a role originally intended for Telly Savalas: the rebellious convict Luke in *Cool Hand Luke*.

A year later, at forty-three, Newman produced and directed his first feature film, *Rachel, Rachel,* casting Joanne Woodward in the lead. For a first attempt, it was masterful, winning four Oscar nominations (including Best Film and Best Actress) and the Golden Globe Award for Best Film.

The following year, in 1969, a film that would become a classic of cinema appeared: *Butch Cassidy and the Sundance Kid,* featuring Paul Newman and Robert Redford as the mythic duo. The producers had originally wanted Steve McQueen, then Marlon Brando, for the role of Butch, but finally offered it to Redford. At Redford's request, however, the roles were switched so that Newman played the part of Butch. Although they are often associated with each other in peoples' minds, Newman and Redford have only made two movies together. They were together again in 1973 in *The Sting*, as Henry Gondorff (Newman) and Johnny Hooker (Redford).

At the height of his career, wishing to spend more of his time with his family, Newman began to distance himself from Hollywood. Nevertheless, he agreed to appear in the disaster film *The Towering Inferno* in 1974, pocketing the record fee of a million dollars and 10 percent of the receipts.

On November 20, 1978, Paul's life took a tragic turn: In a Los Angeles motel, his only son, Scott, died of an overdose of drugs and alcohol at the age of twenty-eight. Devastated, Newman made far fewer films in the 1980s. He replaced Robert Redford on very short notice in the role of the fallen alcoholic lawyer in the Sidney Lumet film *The Verdict* in 1982. Six years after his son's death, he produced *Harry & Son,* a drama about the failure of communication between a father and his son. Two years later, at the request of Martin Scorsese, he agreed to reprise his role from *The Hustler* in *The Color of Money* (1986), alongside a promising young actor named Tom Cruise.

It was *The Color of Money* that earned Paul Newman, after six nominations and thirty-three years in the trade, a well-deserved Oscar. He was sixty-two years old.

PAUL NEWMAN, RACE CAR DRIVER

Newman had discovered his interest in racing during the 1968 shooting of *Winning,* in which he played an Indy 500 driver. In 1972, at the age of forty-seven, he took part in his first car race in Thompson, Connecticut, at the wheel of a Lotus Elan. Four years later he won his first title with his Triumph TR6 at the National Championship of the Sports Car Club of America. The following year, he finished fifth in the grueling 24 Hours of Daytona race.

In 1979, Newman participated in the 24 Hours of Le Mans, finishing in second place at the wheel of his Porsche 935. Fifty-

five years old at the time, he was the oldest racer ever to participate in this prestigious competition.

In 1983, Newman co-founded the Newman-Haas racing team with Carl Haas. Over the years, he could be found at many tracks, especially those at Brainerd, Minnesota, and at Lime Rock Park near his home in Connecticut. In February 1995, at the age of sixty-six, Newman won the title at the 24 Hours of Daytona.

Equally capable as a team manager, in 2003 he hired the services of a young French driver, Sébastien Bourdais, who was voted best rookie during his first season driving the Champ Car circuit. Newman was overjoyed, and in both 2004 and 2005, his prodigious driver carried the title.

Each year, Newman lines up on the starting line to race at Lime Rock or Daytona. He doesn't drive purely for pleasure, however: "the Battler" is out to win. At the age of eighty, Newman managed to finish in the top five in 2005, alongside drivers less than half his age.

PAUL NEWMAN, PHILANTHROPIST

The free-spirited and politically active Newmans have always stood up for their ideals. Together, Paul and Joanne have rallied in support of a variety of political, social, and humanitarian causes, not just as supporters, but as outspoken participants.

After they were married, they were referred to as pioneers for speaking their minds to a shocked Hollywood press. Both were supporters of John F. Kennedy, and Paul campaigned for antiwar candidate Eugene McCarthy. They were also active in the civil rights movement at the side of Martin Luther King Jr. In 1970, they appeared in the documentary film by Sidney Lumet and

Joseph L. Mankiewicz called *King: A Filmed Record . . . Montgomery to Memphis.*

Joanne, for her part, has been an environmental activist and pro-choice advocate, while Paul has lobbied for nuclear disarmament and for gun control. While their political positions have made them some enemies, over the years they have remained faithful to their ideals. After Watergate, Newman was proud to discover that he was included on Richard Nixon's Enemies List.

Paul Newman has established a number of foundations to channel resources to his causes, starting in the 1960s. In 1980, following the death of Paul's son Scott, the couple created the Scott Newman Foundation to combat drug abuse and foster drug and alcohol rehabilitation. Newman created another foundation in 1982: Newman's Own, a line of food products, to which Newman's Own Organics was added in 1993. The profits from products from salad dressings to popcorn to lemonade are dispersed to various organizations; since its inception, Newman's Own has distributed more than $200 million to charitable, educational, and health organizations for children, including the Scott Newman Foundation. Newman also established the Hole in the Wall Gang Camp in 1988, which has since expanded to include a dozen Hole in the Wall Camps for children with life-threatening illnesses. These camps provide children a fun and energizing experience in the care of a well-equipped medical team, at no cost to their families. Over 14,000 children have been able to attend so far.

Today, Newman is more active than ever. Whether at the wheel of his racing cars or at the head of the boardroom table, he maintains his usual place on the front line. In 2002, he returned to the stage for the first time in thirty-five years in *Our Town,* produced by Joanne Woodward in their hometown at the Westport (Connecticut) Country Playhouse. Newman was nominated for a Tony and an Emmy.

Paul Newman also returned to the screen that year in Sam Mendes's *Road to Perdition* (2002), playing an Irish Mafia godfather, mentor to Tom Hanks, a performance for which he was nominated for an Academy Award for Best Actor. He also won an Emmy and a Golden Globe for Outstanding Supporting Actor for his performance in *Empire Falls* (2005). Most recently, he was the voice of "Doc Hudson" in the animated film *Cars* (2006).

What will be this inimitable man's farewell to cinema? Fans await.

—Laurance Aiach

"Once I started taking drama classes, I asked myself why I had ever wasted so much time on a football team."

1964 / Hollywood, CA / Studio portrait of the actor at the age of 39.

1963 / Studio photo of Paul Newman, 38 years old.

1967 / Hollywood, CA / Paul Newman in *Hombre*, directed by Martin Ritt.

1956 / Paul Newman on the set of *Somebody Up There Likes Me*, directed by Robert Wise, in which he played the boxer Rocky Graziano. The role was initially intended for James Dean, who died tragically shortly before filming began.

ABOVE AND OPPOSITE: 1955 / New York, NY / Paul Newman at the Actors Studio. He gained entrance to the prestigious school founded by Lee Strasberg in a highly unusual way: A friend asked him to be her partner for her audition. Paul immediately caught the jury's attention. He was offered admission to the Actors Studio without having to pass the two rounds of juried auditions normally required.

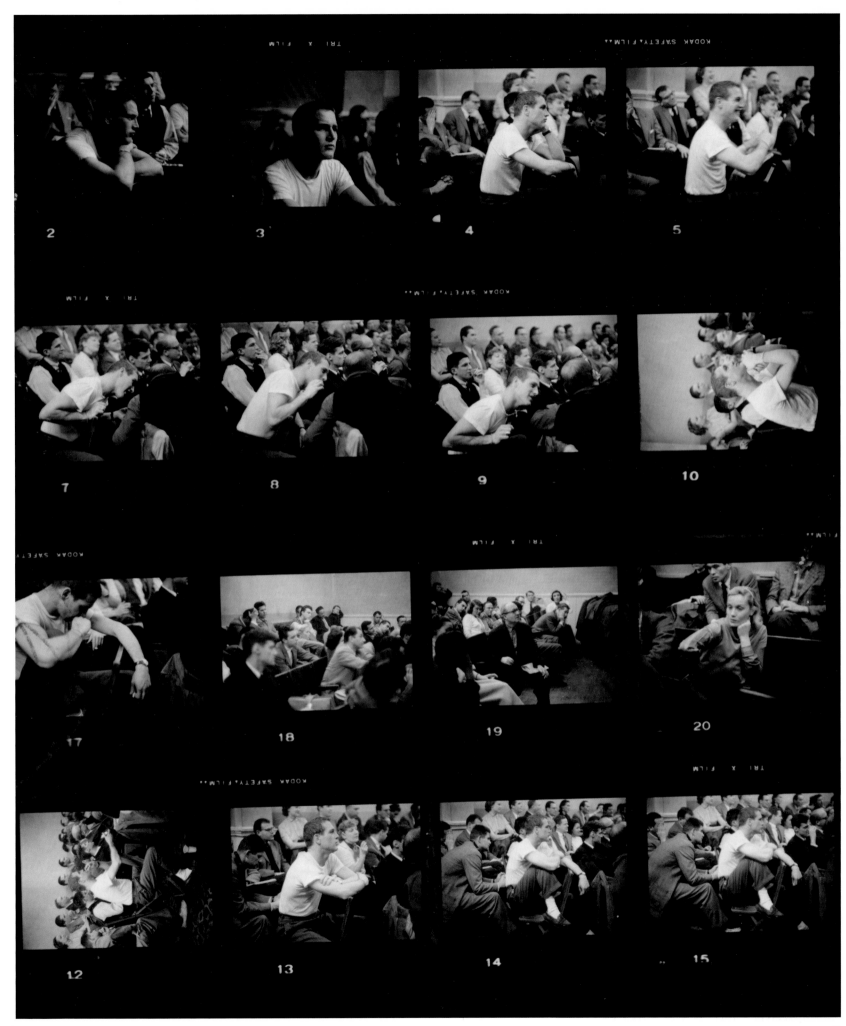

THIS PAGE: January 2, 1960 /
New York, NY / Paul Newman and
Joanne Woodward outside their home
in Greenwich Village.

OPPOSITE: 1958 / Paul and Joanne
studying the script for *The Long, Hot
Summer* directed by Martin Ritt,
in which both of them had parts.

ABOVE: 1962 / Newman was nominated for a Golden Globe for his interpretation of "The Battler" in *Hemingway's Adventures of a Young Man.*
OPPOSITE: January 24, 1956 / Hollywood, CA / While preparing for the role of Rocky Graziano in *Somebody Up There Likes Me*, Paul trained long and hard with former world champion middleweight boxer Tony Zale.

1961 / Paul Newman played billiards champion Eddie Felson in Robert Rossen's *The Hustler*. He would take up this role again forty-five years later in *The Color of Money*, directed by Martin Scorsese, acting alongside Tom Cruise.

NO DOGS OR PETS Allowed in Zoo

1956 / Paul Newman with Louis XIV, photographer Sanford H. Roth's cat.

"Almost everything that I learned about being an actor came from those early years at the Actors Studio."

March 26, 1958 / Joanne Woodward, who had just received the Oscar for Best Actress for *The Three Faces of Eve*, dancing with Paul at the ball following the awards ceremony.

1964 / New York, NY / Paul Newman
captured in a photograph in the
costume he wore in the Broadway play
Baby Want a Kiss, which he performed
148 times in 1964.

—"What's the secret to your marriage [to Joanne Woodward]?"
—"I don't know what she puts in my food."

PRECEDING PAGES:
1958 / Beverly Hills, CA / Paul Newman
and Joanne Woodward at their home in
California, admiring the Oscar for Best
Actress that Joanne had just won for her
role in *The Three Faces of Eve*, and the
imitation Oscar that friends of Paul's
offered him as consolation. Newman would
be nominated for Best Actor no less than
six times, without success, before being
awarded the coveted award for his part in
The Color of Money in 1986.

January 29, 1958 / The wedding of
Paul Newman and Joanne Woodward.

PRECEDING PAGES : 1961 / Paris, France / Paul Newman and Joanne Woodward in *Paris Blues*, directed by Martin Ritt.

1961 / Paul Newman in Robert Rossen's *The Hustler*.

1965 / Nice, France / Paul Newman in
Lady L, a film by Peter Ustinov in which
he and Sophia Loren shared top billing.

ABOVE AND OPPOSITE: January 29, 1965 / Paul Newman and his children on vacation in France.

"Every time I get a script it's a matter of trying to know what I could do with it. I see colors, imagery. It has to have a smell. It's like falling in love. You can't give a reason why."

OPPOSITE AND ABOVE: 1963 / Claude, TX / Paul Newman during the filming of *Hud*, directed by Martin Ritt.

ABOVE AND OPPOSITE: 1962 / In the middle of the desert, Paul Newman interacts with some vultures during the filming of *Hud*.

OPPOSITE: 1958 / Paul Newman during the filming of *The Left Handed Gun*, written by his friend Gore Vidal and directed by Arthur Penn.
ABOVE: 1967 / Paul Newman in Martin Ritt's *Hombre*.

"Acting is a question of absorbing other people's personalities and adding some of your own experience."

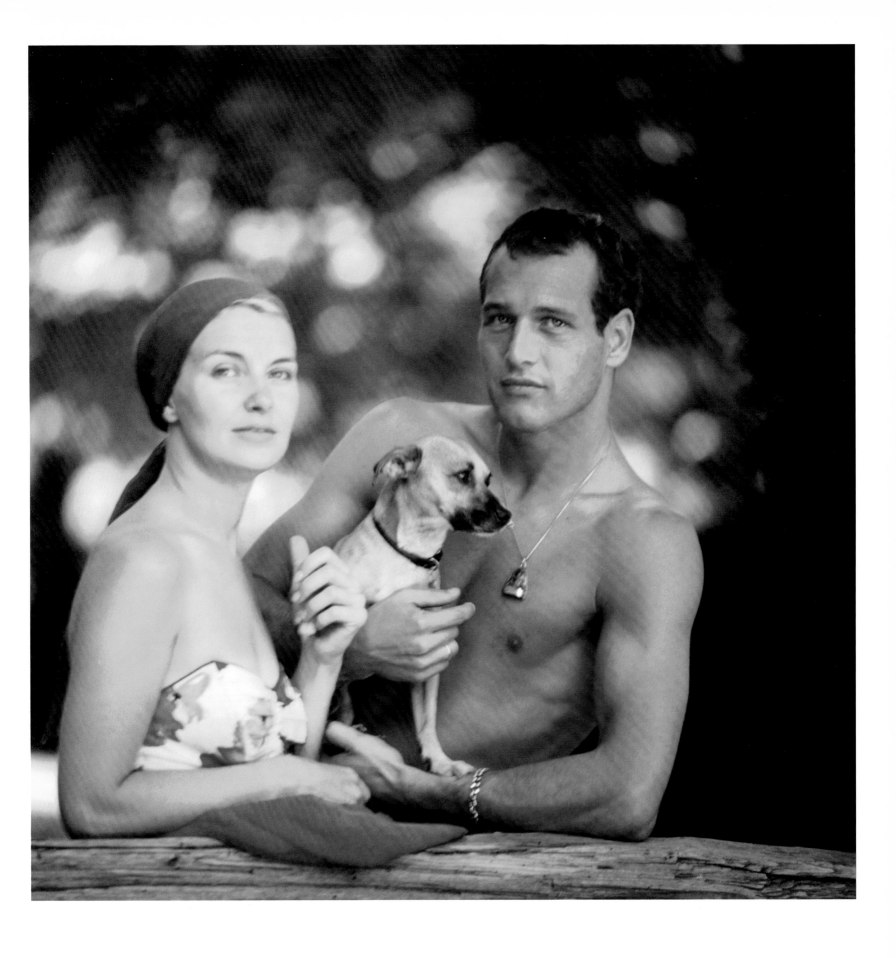

PRECEDING PAGES: 1963 / Paul Newman in *The Prize*, directed by Mark Robson.

1963 / Westport, CT / Paul Newman, Joanne Woodward, and their dog.

1963 / Joanne Woodward panicking as her dress comes undone during the filming of Melville Shavelson's *A New Kind of Love*.
1960 / Paul Newman on a Vespa.

1965 / Hollywood, CA / Paul on the set of the 1966 film *Harper*, directed by Jack Smight.

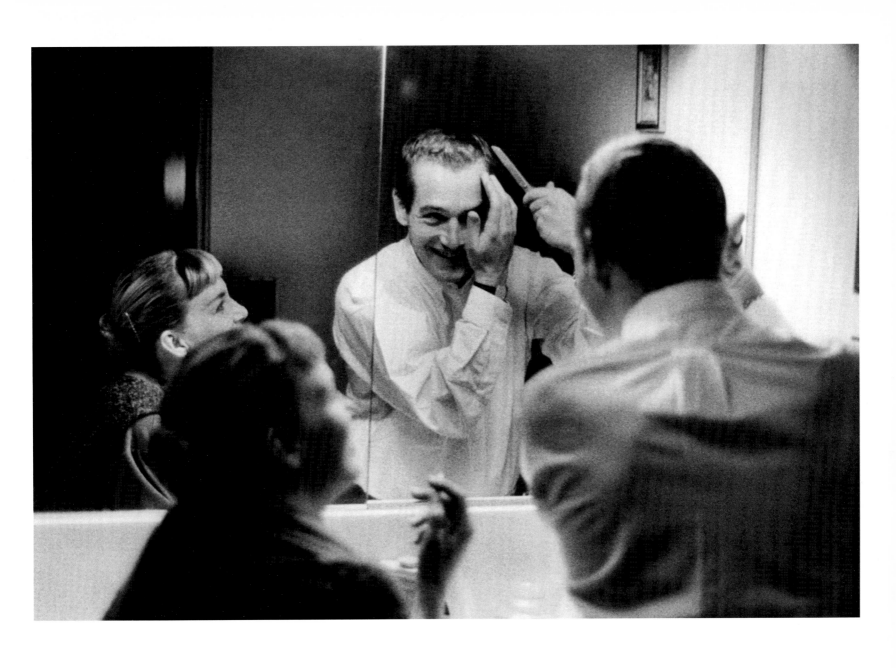

March 1, 1959 / Paul Newman and Joanne Woodward in a dressing room getting ready for their stage entrance.

"I picture my epitaph: 'Here lies Paul Newman, who died a failure because his eyes turned brown.'"

September 28, 1986 / Conversation with *New York Times* journalist Maureen Dowd

1970 / Hollywood, CA / Studio portrait
of Paul Newman.

June 14, 1972 / New York, NY / Paul Newman in Madison Square Garden, surrounded by a horde of his fans.

May 25, 1963 / Hollywood, CA / Paul Newman and Joanne Woodward after adding their handprints and footprints to those on Hollywood Boulevard, near Grauman's Chinese Theater. They were the 140th and 141st people to take part in this celebrated Hollywood ritual.

"Acting isn't really a creative profession. It's an interpretative one."

1960 / Paris, France / Paul Newman on the set of *Paris Blues*, directed by Martin Ritt.

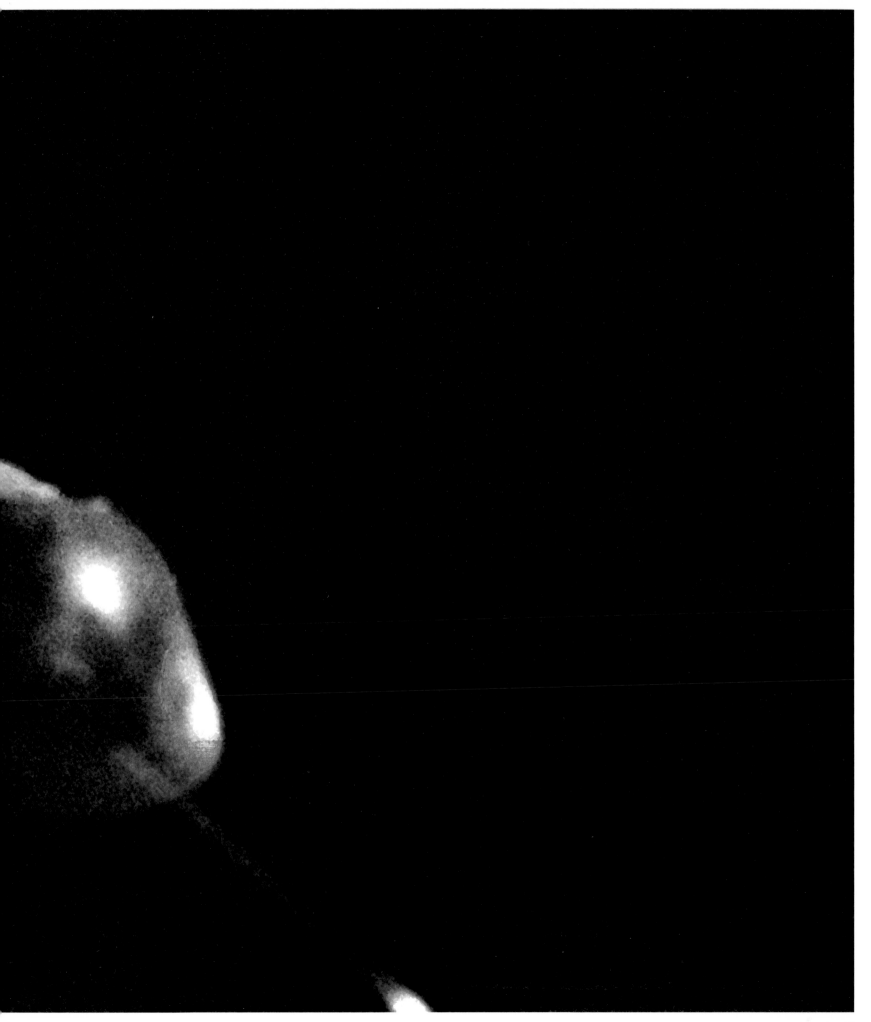

PRECEDING PAGES: 1964 / Paul Newman during a fencing lesson while preparing for *Lady L*, directed by Peter Ustinov.

June 30, 1960 / Paris, France / Paul Newman with Martin Ritt, director of *Paris Blues*.

1960 / Paris, France / Paul Newman in *Paris Blues*.

1960 / Paris, France / Louis Armstrong, Paul Newman, and Duke Ellington during the filming of *Paris Blues*.

1960 / Paris, France / Newman during the filming of *Paris Blues*.
FOLLOWING PAGES: November 2, 1960 / Paris, France / Paul and Joanne in their apartment on Montmartre several weeks before the filming of *Paris Blues*.

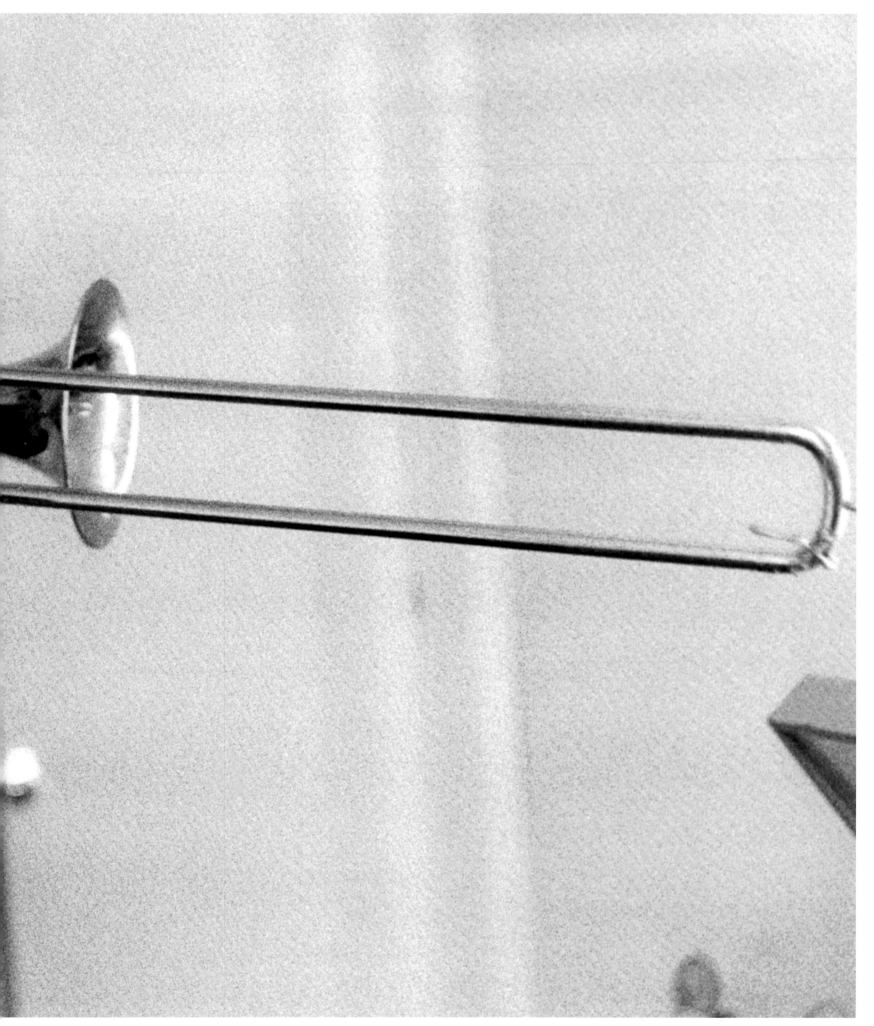

THIS SPREAD: 1964 / Paul and Joanne
clown around at home.

"People stay married because they want to, not because the doors are locked."

—from *Winning* (1969)

PRECEDING PAGES: 1963 / Paul Newman and Joanne Woodward improvise a photo session at home.

1963 / Hollywood, CA / Paul and Joanne during the filming of *A New Kind of Love*, directed by Melville Shavelson.

"In the early days of films, the movie star in this country replaced royalty . . . They've been demoted since then but they're still treated like beings larger than life."

PRECEDING PAGES: 1958 / Beverly Hills, CA / Paul Newman and Joanne Woodward at home.

1965 / Hollywood, CA / Portrait of Paul Newman at the age of 40.

78

THIS PAGE: September 19, 1969 / Utah /
On the set of *Butch Cassidy and the
Sundance Kid*, directed by George Roy Hill.

OPPOSITE: 1969 / Paul Newman
and Robert Redford in
Butch Cassidy and the Sundance Kid.

"The characters I have the least in common with are the ones I have the greatest success with. The further a role is from my own experience, the more I try to deepen it."

1969 / Paul Newman and Robert Redford in *Butch Cassidy and the Sundance Kid.*

PRECEDING PAGES: 1967 / Melissa Newman enjoys a laugh with director Martin Ritt on the set of *Hombre*, as the cast jokes around.

1967 / Paul Newman in Stuart Rosenberg's *Cool Hand Luke*.

1967 / Paul Newman in *Cool Hand Luke.*

"To be an actor, you have to be a child."

May 17, 1965 / Westport, CT / Paul Newman and Joanne Woodward at their home in Connecticut.

May 17, 1965 / Westport, CT / Paul and Joanne in the yard of their home.

"Men experience many passions in a lifetime. One passion drives away the one before it."

PRECEDING PAGES: May 17, 1965 / Westport, CT / Paul and Joanne on a fishing trip.

1965 / Hollywood, CA / Paul Newman with his daughter, Claire.

94

1965 / Hollywood, CA / Paul Newman with
his daughters Melissa and Elinor
at their home in California.

1968 / Riverside, CA / Paul Newman and his daughter Elinor during the filming of the 1969 movie *Winning*, directed by James Goldstone.

OPPOSITE: 1966 / Hollywood, CA / Paul Newman and Alfred Hitchcock on the set of *Torn Curtain*, produced by Universal Studios.

THIS PAGE: 1968 / Danbury, CT / Paul Newman during the filming of *Rachel, Rachel*, his debut film as a director. He cast his wife, Joanne Woodward, in the lead role. The film was nominated for four Oscars, including Best Film and Best Actress, and won two Golden Globe Awards: Best Performance by an Actress and Best Director.

PRECEDING PAGES: 1968 / On the set of *Rachel, Rachel*. His work earned him a Golden Globe and an Oscar nomination.

August 27, 1963 / Washington, DC / Paul Newman arriving to participate in the March on Washington, a massive civil rights demonstration held the following day.

March 28, 1968 / Minneapolis, MN / Paul Newman demonstrates with students to encourage support for Wisconsin senator Eugene McCarthy's campaign.

"I don't go for fancy talk about the mystique of speed, I drive for the hell of it."

1969 / Indianapolis, IN / Paul Newman in *Winning*, directed by James Goldstone.

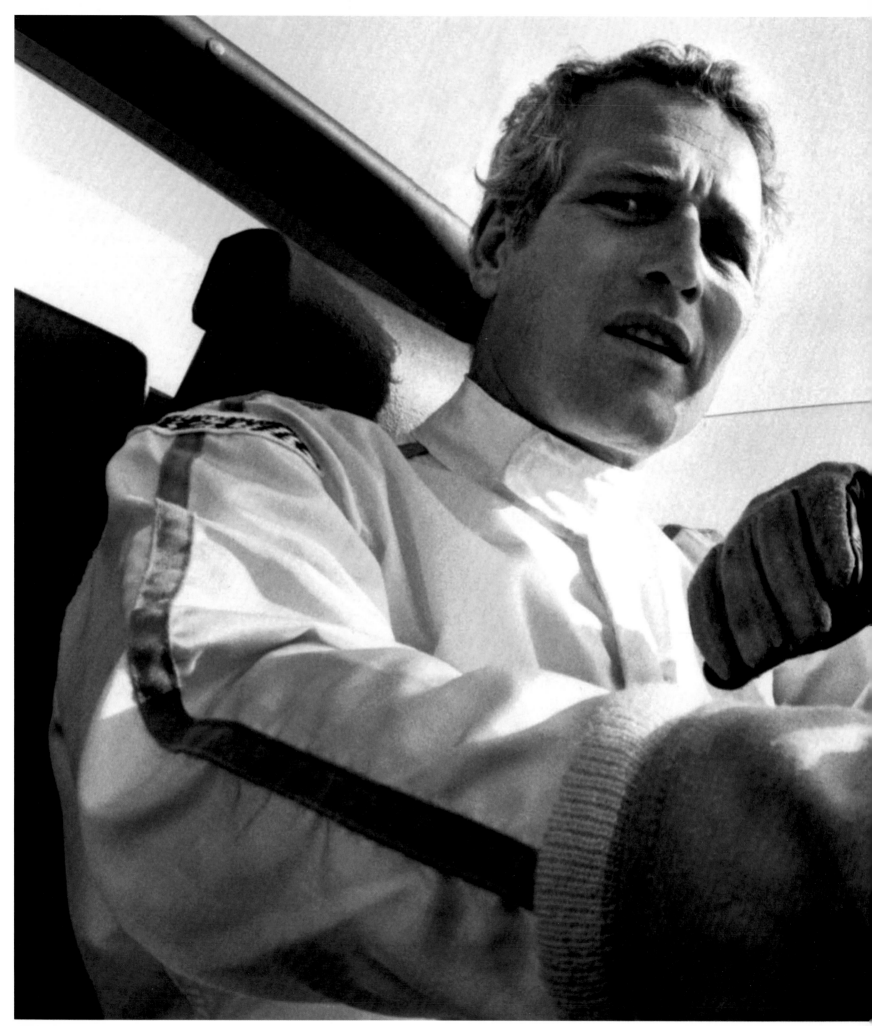

PRECEDING PAGES: 1969 / Indianapolis, IN / Paul Newman at the wheel of a race car in *Winning*.

June 17, 1968 / Indianapolis, IN / Paul Newman in conversation with the technical consultant for *Winning*, two-time Indianapolis 500 champion Roger Ward.

1969 / Paul Newman in *Winning*. Newman discovered his passion for car racing while making this film, which would lead him to race in many professional circuits, participate in the 24 Hours of Le Mans, and to become co-owner of the Newman-Haas Champ Car racing team, two-time world champions in 2004 and 2005.

"Money won is twice as sweet as money earned."

—from *The Color of Money* (1986)

1971 / Paul Newman in *Sometimes a Great Notion*, a film he also directed.

ABOVE AND OPPOSITE: 1969 / Paul Newman and Joanne Woodward during the filming of *Winning*.

OPPOSITE: 1970 / Paul and Joanne take a break while shooting *WUSA*, a film directed by Stuart Rosenberg and coproduced by Newman.
ABOVE: 1969 / Paul and Joanne relax on the beach during the filming of James Goldstone's *Winning*.

PRECEDING PAGES: 1970 / Paul and Joanne during the filming of Stuart Rosenberg's *WUSA*.

September 9, 1968 / Paul, Joanne, and their daughter Elinor.

1967 / Keys, FL / Paul Newman on the set of his film, *Rachel, Rachel*.

"A man with no enemies is a man with no character."

1970 / Paul Newman on the set of *WUSA*, a film he coproduced in addition to costarring with Joanne Woodward and Anthony Perkins.

120

1974 / Hollywood, CA / Paul Newman and Steve McQueen in *The Towering Inferno*, directed by John Guillermin and Irwin Allen. For that film, Paul pocketed a record fee at the time: a million dollars plus 10% of gross receipts.

1967 / Hollywood, CA / Paul Newman was 42 when he played the title role in *Cool Hand Luke.*

PRECEDING PAGES: 1974 / Group photo of the principal actors in *The Towering Inferno*: Robert Wagner, Fred Astaire, Richard Chamberlain, Paul Newman, William Holden, Faye Dunaway, Steve McQueen, Jennifer Jones, O.J. Simpson, and Robert Vaughn.

September 22, 1972 / Hollywood, CA / Steve McQueen, Paul Newman, Barbra Streisand, and Sidney Poitier celebrate the creation of their own production and distribution agency, First Artists Production Company.

January 16, 1974 / New York, NY / While filming *The Sting*, director George Roy Hill relaxes with the two stars, Paul Newman and Robert Redford. *The Sting* is the second and last film in which the two actors played together, following *Butch Cassidy and the Sundance Kid*.

ABOVE AND OPPOSITE: 1975 / Louisiana / Paul Newman reprised his famous 1966 role in *Harper* as Lew Harper in the film *The Drowning Pool*.

ABOVE: April 3, 1968 / New York, NY / Paul Newman, his daughters Susan and Melissa, and his wife, Joanne Woodward, at the premiere of *2001: A Space Odyssey*, directed by Stanley Kubrick.
OPPOSITE: January 26, 1969 / New York, NY / Paul Newman and Joanne Woodward during the award ceremony of the New York Film Critics Circle.

"Car racing is the first thing I have ever found that I had any grace in."

March 18, 1977 / Sebring, FL / Paul Newman qualified for the 12 Hours of Sebring in his Porsche 911. His helmet bears his blood type (O+), his age (52), the date of his last tetanus vaccination (1975), and a note indicating that he has no allergies.

1979 / Paul Newman between two rounds
of trials.

OPPOSITE: July 3, 1982 / Lime Rock Park, CT / In the stands during the Kendall Cup auto race.

THIS PAGE: May 2, 1976 / New York, NY / Paul has a good laugh during a press conference marking the release of *Buffalo Bill and the Indians, or Sitting Bull's History Lesson*, directed by Robert Altman.

1960 / Westport, CT / Paul enjoying
a light-hearted game of tennis.

1974 / White Mountain National Forest, NH / Paul, Joanne, and their daughters Melissa (left) and Claire Olivia (right) participating in a documentary, *The Wild Places*, that aired on NBC. The entire Newman family appeared in the program, hiking through the most spectacular American parks.

1974 / White Mountain National Forest, NH / Paul and his daughter Claire Olivia, age 9, during the filming of *The Wild Places*.

1974 / White Mountain National Forest,
NH / Paul Newman and Joanne Woodward
during the making of the NBC program
The Wild Places.

"I would like it if people would think that beyond Newman, there's a spirit that takes action, a heart, and a talent that doesn't come from my blue eyes."

1976 / Portrait of Paul Newman at the age of 51.

THIS PAGE: July 6, 1975 / Lime Rock, CT /
Paul Newman, who had just finished
second in a car race at Lime Rock Park,
joins his team and his fans.

OPPOSITE: May 7, 1980 / Lime Rock, CT /
Paul Newman on the circuit at Lime Rock.

THIS PAGE: 1975 /
Newman on a ski vacation.

OPPOSITE: August 13, 1987 /
Westport, CT / Paul playing in a baseball
game to raise money for his Hole in the
Wall summer camps. These camps,
founded by Newman, give seriously ill
children the opportunity to enjoy a
summer camp experience with all kinds of
activities while under the care of medical
specialists, at no cost to their families.

ABOVE: 1977 / Paul Newman as a hockey player/coach in *Slap Shot*, directed by George Roy Hill.
OPPOSITE: 1973 / Buckinghamshire, England / Paul Newman on the set of the John Huston film *The Mackintosh Man* at Pinewood Studios.

"I am not an intuitive actor. I direct myself. I suppose that makes me more of a director than an actor."

CAMERA

November 20, 1978

PRECEDING PAGES: 1972 / London, England / Paul Newman fights his way through a crowd of admirers at the end of a shoot.

158

1975 / Portrait of Scott Newman made during the filming of *The Towering Inferno*, in which he played alongside his father.

OPPOSITE: July 5, 1980 / Lime Rock, CT / Test run on the race track at Lime Rock.

THIS PAGE: June 9, 1979 / Le Mans, France / Paul Newman at the 24 Hours of Le Mans race. Driving a Porsche 935 prepared by Dick Barbour, owner of the team, he and co-drivers Barbour and Rolf Stommelen finished in second place.

"I will continue to get behind the wheel of a racing car as long as I am able. But that could all end tomorrow...."

June 9, 1979 / Le Mans, France / Paul Newman at the 24 Hours of Le Mans race.

THIS PAGE AND OPPOSITE: June 9, 1979 / Le Mans, France / Newman at the 24 Hours of Le Mans.

164

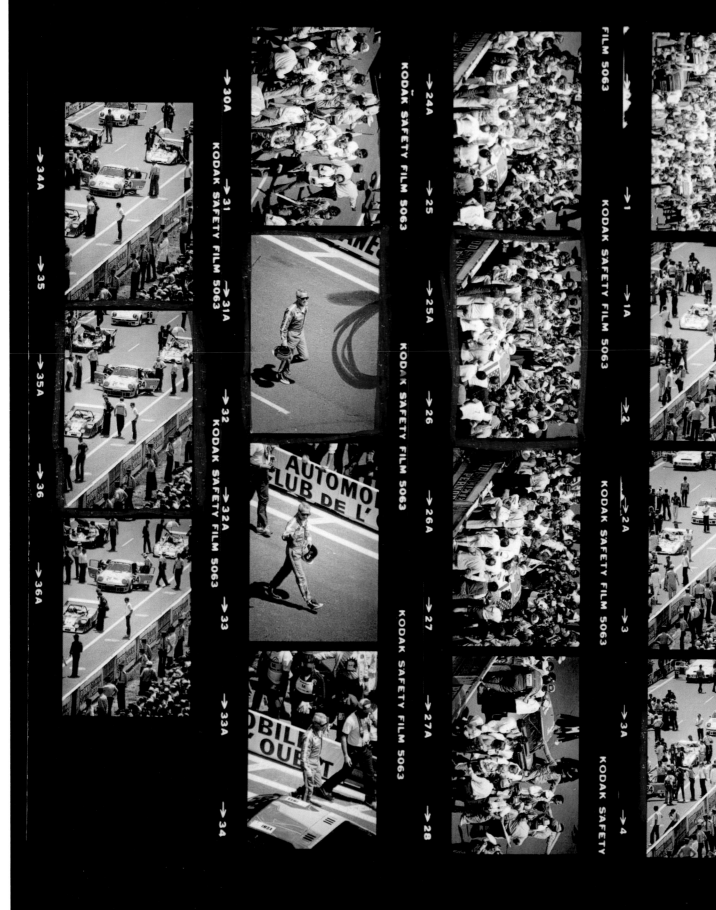

"A man can only be judged by his actions, and not by his good intentions or his beliefs."

May 31, 1978 / New York, NY / Invited to appear on the NBC television program *Today*, Paul Newman spoke about his function as a special delegate to a United Nations General Assembly session devoted to disarmament. In the background, Newman can be seen with the American delegation next to Senator George McGovern.

UNITED STATES

PRECEDING PAGES: May 26, 1978 / New York, NY / Paul Newman is one of many celebrities actively involved in political causes. Here he participates in a special session of the General Assembly of the United Nations on disarmament.

February 18, 1977 / New York, NY / Paul in a restaurant on Broadway.

October 1980 / Beverly Hills, CA /
Portrait of Paul Newman at the age of 55.

July 12, 1987 / Lexington, OH / Newman supervises the preparation of his car at the SCCA (Sports Car Club of America) Bendix Trans Am Race.

April 26, 1981 / Riverside, CA / Newman
at the six-hour Los Angeles Times/Toyota
Grand Prix of Endurance event.

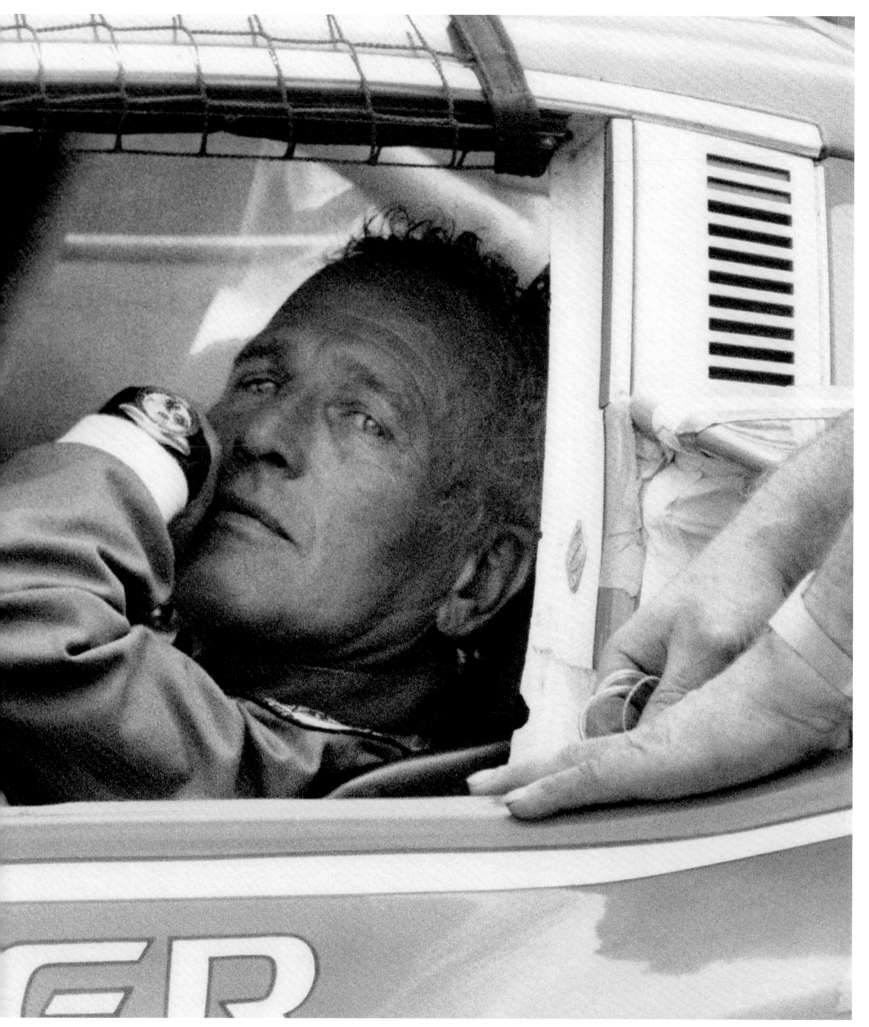

PRECEDING PAGES: April 26, 1981 / Riverside, CA / Paul Newman unwinds before departing from the LA Times/Toyota Grand Prix of Endurance.

June 9, 1979 / Le Mans, France / Newman takes a few moments to concentrate before the start of the 24 Hours of Le Mans.

February 6, 1977 / Daytona Beach, FL / Paul Newman at the wheel of his Ferrari on the track during the 24 Hours of Daytona, the first professional race he had participated in as an amateur.

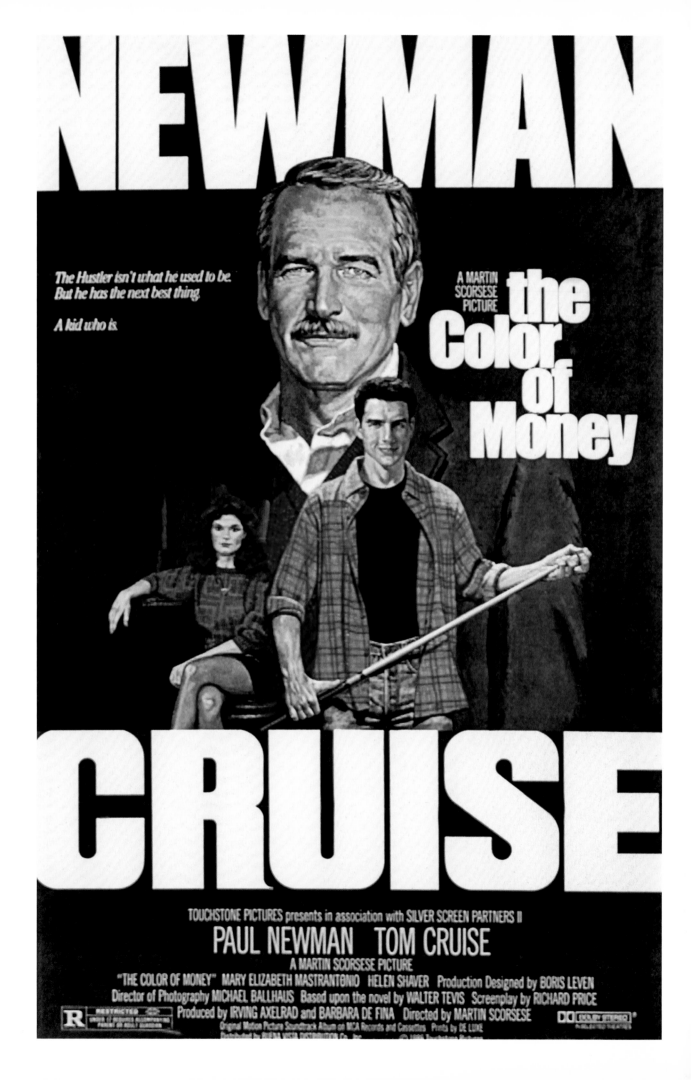

1986 / Poster for *The Color of Money*, directed by Martin Scorsese. Paul Newman received the Oscar for Best Actor for this movie, after being nominated six times over the course of his thirty-three year career in acting at that point. He shared top billing with Tom Cruise, at the time a young actor of 23, whose career took off with the great success of *Top Gun*, released the same year.

January 29, 1984 / Los Angeles, CA / Paul Newman received the Cecil B. de Mille Award at the Golden Globe Awards, honoring his outstanding contributions to the field of entertainment throughout his career.

June 1987 / England / Elinor Newman, Paul's daughter, presenting a check to the Double O charity, an organization that helps abused children. It was founded by Pete Townshend, guitarist for The Who.

1985 / New York, NY / Paul Newman presents the line of salad dressings that bear his name, Newman's Own, "the star of oil and vinegar and the oil and vinegar of the stars." Created in 1982, Newman's Own is a non-profit organization that donates all its profits to charitable causes. Paul Newman has distributed more than 200 million dollars since the founding of Newman's Own.

May 12, 1987 / Cannes, France /
Paul Newman and Joanne Woodward make
their entrance at the Cannes Festival.

July 1984 / Cambridge, MA / Paul Newman, age 59, worked side by side with Congresswoman Patricia Schroeder, co-president of the GGAC (Gender Gap Action Campaign). In that year, the GGAC, an organization that defends the rights of women, led an active campaign against Ronald Reagan's reelection to the White House.

"I don't think that there's anything exceptional or noble in being philanthropic. It's the other attitude that confuses me."

January 23, 1992 / Paul Newman backstage after attending a Broadway performance of the play *Park Your Car in Harvard Yard*.

THIS PAGE: May 25, 1990 / Bronxville, NY / Paul Newman at Sarah Lawrence College, where he is about to deliver the commencement address.

OPPOSITE: October 24, 1983 / New York, NY / Newman at a benefit concert in Avery Fisher Hall at Lincoln Center to support artistic efforts against nuclear proliferation.

"As long as my heart continues to beat, I think I will continue."

May 19, 1983 / Indianapolis, IN /
Paul Newman at the Indianapolis track to
watch his driver, Mario Andretti (left), in
the trials.

190

PRECEDING PAGES: September 13, 1981 / South Hampton, NY / Paul Newman and his technician at the start of the Bridgehampton circuit.

ABOVE AND OPPOSITE: July 5, 1980 / Lime Rock, CT / Paul Newman savoring his victory on the track at Lime Rock.

November 7, 2004 / Mexico City, Mexico / Group photo of the Newman-Haas team including the drivers, Sébastien Bourdais (left) and Bruno Junqueira (right), co-founders Paul Newman and Carl Haas, and the crew. The Newman-Haas team had just claimed victory on the Hermanos Rodriguez Racetrack, thereby clinching the title of Champ Car World Series Champions for 2004.

November 7, 2004 / Mexico City, Mexico / Sébastien Bourdais, the French driver for the Newman-Haas team, brandishing the victory flag at the last Grand Prix of the season, at the Hermanos Rodriguez Racetrack. He captured his first Champ Car World Series championship title that year.

July 30, 2000 / Cicero, IL / Paul Newman and Carl Haas, co-founders of the Newman-Haas team, celebrating the second-place finish scored by their driver, Michael Andretti, in the Target Grand Prix at the Chicago Motor Speedway.

November 7, 2004 / Portland, OR / Paul Newman and driver Sébastien Bourdais celebrate the Newman-Haas team's victory in the Champ Car World Series of Mexico, held at the Hermanos Rodriguez Racetrack.

"I'd like to be remembered as a guy who tried—tried to be part of his times, tried to help people communicate with one another, tried to find some decency in his own life, tried to extend himself as a human being. Someone who isn't complacent, who doesn't cop out."

September 3, 2004 / Kildare, Ireland / Paul Newman on the track at the international Mondello Park Racing Circuit in Ireland, on the occasion of the tenth anniversary of the Hole in the Wall Camp established in Barretstown Castle.

ABOVE AND OPPOSITE: August 11, 2004 / Westport, CT / Paul Newman at his home in Connecticut.

ABOVE AND OPPOSITE: 2001 / Barretstown, Ireland / Paul Newman the philanthropist, near the Hole in the Wall Camp at Barretstown Castle that he financed in its entirety. More than 11,000 children from 22 countries have already participated since the camp was opened in 1994.

ABOVE AND OPPOSITE: 2000 / Westport, CT / Portraits of Paul Newman made for *Esquire* magazine around the time that *Empire Falls*, a film made for HBO, was released.

First published in the United States in 2006 by Chronicle Books LLC.
First published in France in 2006 by Editons PHYB.

Copyright © 2006 by Editons PHYB.
Biographical essay copyright © 2006 by Laurence Aiach.
Text copyright © 2006 by Yann-Brice Dherbier and Pierre-Henri Verlhac.
English translation copyright © 2006 by Chronicle Books LLC.
Page 208 constitutes a continuation of the copyright page.

Library of Congress Cataloging-in-Publication Data available.

ISBN-10: 0-8118-5726-3
ISBN-13: 978-0-8118-5726-0

Manufactured in Italy.

Translated and typeset by A-P-E Int'l.
Rolex is gratefully acknowledged for its support of this project

Distributed in Canada by Raincoast Books
9050 Shaughnessy Street
Vancouver, British Columbia V6P 6E5

10 9 8 7 6 5 4 3 2 1

Chronicle Books LLC
680 Second Street
San Francisco, CA 94107

www.chroniclebooks.com